Walks in the Surrey Hills

3rd (Revised) Edition

Compiled by

JANET SPAYNE & AUDREY KRYNSKI
of The Ramblers Association
Croydon & District Group

SPURBOOKS

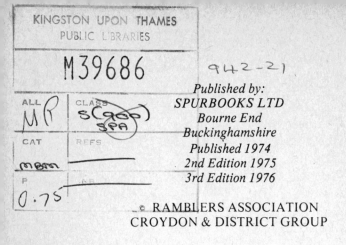

Published by:
SPURBOOKS LTD
Bourne End
Buckinghamshire
Published 1974
2nd Edition 1975
3rd Edition 1976

© RAMBLERS ASSOCIATION
CROYDON & DISTRICT GROUP

S B N   O 902875 82 5

*At the time of publication all the walks in this book were made
along paths designated as official footpaths, but it should be
borne in mind that deviation orders may be made from time to
time.*

Printed by Maund & Irvine Ltd., Tring, Herts.

Contents

Also in
this series

Walks along the South Downs Way (2nd edn.)
Walks along The Ridgeway (1975)
Walks in South Essex
Walks in The New Forest (1975)
Walks in Hertfordshire (1975)
Chiltern Round Walks
Walks West of London
Midland Walks
Walks in the Hills of Kent
Walks in the Cotswolds

Introduction

WE HAVE compiled this collection of walks from an intimate knowledge of the North Downs area acquired over the last five or six years through exploring the countryside together, having met as fellow members of the Ramblers Association. Our rambling activities have opened up a new world for us, giving us an interest in map-reading, in the changing seasons, each of which has its own particular advantages, in animal and insect life and, above all, in plant life. Identification of an unusual flower or tree leads us to reference books and not merely increases our knowledge but our interest in the beautiful countryside of Surrey.

Surrey has some of the widest variety of country to be found in England — farmland, heathland, woods, water and downland and a large number of areas of outstanding natural beauty. The walks in this book explore only a small part of Surrey and for the most part we have avoided the well-trodden ways to share some of the smaller more obscure paths which we have discovered in our wanderings. Sheets 186 and 187 of the new O.S. 1:50.000 maps will cover all the walks but a $2\frac{1}{2}''$ map gives a lot more detail and although not essential will greatly add to your enjoyment in following the routes. The sketch maps included in the text are not to any scale but merely give a rough indication of the direction of the walks.

To any who feel themselves afflicted with middle age boredom when family ties are no longer so demanding, we heartily recommend that they take up rambling and, as we do, set aside a regular day each week to explore the countryside, ideally with one or two friends. For those of all ages we recommend this stimulating occupation as an antidote to the stresses and strains of modern urban life.

AUDREY KRYNSKI
JANET SPAYNE

The Silent Pool

**St. Martha's, Chilworth
6 miles (or two walks of 3 miles each)**

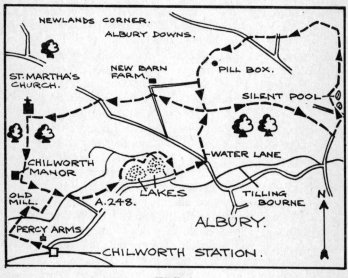

Walk 1

THIS ramble in the Tillingbourne Valley takes us through woodland, downland and farmland. We see the remains of the gunpowder industry for which Chilworth was once famous and pass the mill ponds with their wild life. Very little mud will be encountered.

How to get there: 425 and 439 bus from Dorking to the junction of A.25 and A.248. Or by train to Chilworth where the walk can be joined. By car to the car park at The Silent Pool.

If Chilworth is the starting point

Leaving Chilworth Station we turn left along the main road for approximately 100 yards when we take a footpath on the right next to a school. We cross a bridge over the river, taking the right fork to a crossing track where we turn right, keeping straight ahead to a high bank of earth. Now we continue the walk from (X).

If only a 3 mile walk from Chilworth is desired

Follow the walk to (B) and then turn to (A) — the signposted bridleway on the right referred to at (A) is of course the same left path at (B).

If only a 3 mile walk from The Silent Pool is desired

Follow the walk to (A) and then turn to (C) — the left hand turning at (A) is of course the same right hand turning at (C).

If returning to Chilworth Station or needing Chilworth for refreshment at (X) instead of turning left by the bank of earth, we continue forward and where the woods open out we take the first turning on the left to a bridge over the river continuing on a footpath up to the road by a school. Here we turn left for *The Percy Arms* and Chilworth Station.

Starting from The Silent Pool

After visiting The Silent Pool, which is fed by strong under ground springs and very deep, we return to the entrance and turn right on the track with the Pool on our right, going uphill for nearly half a mile to a wide crossing track at the top of the hill where we turn left. When this forks we take the left, slightly downhill track, and keep left again at the next fork. At this point views of Hascombe Hill can be seen on the skyline. We come out to a road which we cross slightly right to a small footpath, turning right and taking the left of two almost parallel paths, at first keeping parallel with the road on our right. At a junction of paths, with a pillbox on the left, we turn left down a stony track, bearing left just past an old quarry, and continue down the lane passing a turning on the right which goes to New Barn Farm.

(A) A few yards past a turning on the left we take the sign-posted bridleway on the right, going through a gate and along the edge of a field. At the end of the field we turn right along the hedge to a gate on the left into a lane. We take the track opposite with a blue waymark and continue along this Pilgrims' trackway between wooden fences out to a road. We cross the road to a path slightly to the left and go left with it, turning right between posts and going uphill, ignoring all branching paths until St. Martha's Church is reached.

The original church dated from the late 12th century but fell into disrepair and was rebuilt on its original foundations in the mid-19th century.

Leaving the church by the south wicket gate between conifers, opposite the entrance to the church, we take a steep downhill path after ignoring a crossing track. At the end of this footpath we turn right to look at Chilworth Manor. There is a local legend that a tunnel once ran between the Manor and St. Martha's Church. Retrace the few yards and continue along the signposted bridleway which eventually becomes a lane. Just after passing Long Furrow Farm entrance on the left we go through a wicket gate on the right into woods, turning left by a high bank of earth.

(X)   We keep on this path with the Tillingbourne on our right, and on our left we pass the ruins of a gunpowder mill with trees growing up from ground floors to a height well above roof level. From mid 17th century until the end of the first world war Chilworth was an important centre for the gunpowder industry. These woods are full of old mill stones and remains of other mills, and in the 1914-18 war a regiment of soldiers kept guard day and night on the various buildings.

Passing the mill buildings on our left we return to the lane where we turn right over the bridge and immediately left over a stile. We cross a meadow diagonally right to another stile, turning left and parallel with a wet ditch on our right, then over another stile and plank bridge into a field, keeping straight ahead with a wire fence on the right. Another stile takes us into a private garden which has the public footpath running close to the fence on the right. We come out into a lane where we turn left and round the edge of the lake passing a mill. The path bears left at the end of the first lake round to another lake. We turn right at the cottage by a rising footpath with the lake on our right, then through an iron barrier, keeping forward on the footpath through cottage gardens and out into the main road.

We turn left in the road and take the second turning on the left into Water Lane. We go along here for about half a mile to a signpost on the left (B) and just beyond is a turning to the right (C) which we take, passing a few houses. This becomes a grassy track and passes an isolated cottage on the right. We continue forward and where the track forks we take a small path in the trees between the forks. At the end of this path we cross a sandy track to a small path opposite with a wooden hut on the right. We bear right behind the hut with a fence on the left and soon climb over a stile on the left. Following the fence across a field we come to a road where we turn left and are soon at the main road which we cross to the house at the entrance to The Silent Pool.

Refreshments: Cafe at The Silent Pool and an inn at Chilworth.

Chilworth

**Chilworth, Shamley Green, Wonersh
6¾ miles**

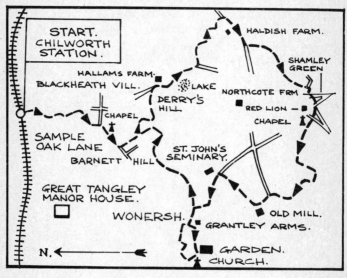

Walk 2

THIS is a ramble in woodland and over heather and gorse covered heathland, visiting two of Surrey's pretty villages, Shamley Green and Wonersh, with their 16th and 17th century houses. The walk is recommended for any time of the year and while there are bluebells in spring and heather in high summer, it is perhaps at its best on a crisp winter day with hoar frost on the ground.

How to get there: By train or No. 425 or 439 bus to Chilworth

Station. By car on the A.248 (off the A.25) turning left by Chilworth Station up Sampleoak Lane to a car parking space at the top of the hill on the right opposite the *Blackheath* sign.

From the station we turn left up Sampleoak Lane for about half a mile. There is a parallel footpath on the left of the road. We pass a Franciscan Friary on the right and walk to the top of the hill to a small car parking space opposite the *Blackheath* sign.

From the car park we take the small right diagonal path to the south-west across a heather-covered common. At a T junction we turn right into a wider sandy track soon coming to a crossing track where we turn left and then straight ahead, ignoring a right fork, till the path bears left, passes some houses and leads us out to a road. Here we turn right and at the end of the houses on the left and at the *Blackheath* sign we turn left. In about 25 yards, as this lane bears left to go behind some houses, we take a small path on the right with fields on the right behind the hedge. Very soon we take the first very small path on the left, initially lined with holly bushes, uphill to the top of Derry's Hill. The path bears right taking us along the ridge of the hill, **giving extensive views to Hascombe Hill on the right and St. Martha's Church on the hill on the left.**

At the wide T junction we turn right and in about 100 yards as the track turns left between young pines we turn right and in a couple of yards turn left under taller pine trees, keeping ahead to a crossing track and a wire fence round a plantation which we keep on our right as we go along a sandy track. This later bears left downhill becoming a sunken path which we follow with the fence on our right until we reach a minor road. We turn right along the road and just past farm buildings we take the signposted footpath to Darbyns Brook, passing the picturesque Hallams Farm on the left. Continuing along the gravel drive we turn right past a lake and left past a beautiful house where we turn right through a white gate along a hedged track. This brings us out to a tarmac lane where we turn right passing the attractive Haldish Farm on our right.

At Blackmoor Lodge we take a signposted footpath on the left between high fences, then go over a stile to a path just inside a wood with open fields on our left. We go over another stile and

11

in a few yards, when the path forks, we take the right fork and again after a few yards, the next left fork, going uphill through bracken and open woodland of oak and birch, following the main small path on the ridge of Reelhall Hill to a main track. We turn right and cross another wider track almost immediately to a holly bush on our left. We take the first left of two paths and go straight ahead downhill through bracken, ignoring any turnings, through a wicket gate into a field. We cross the field with the hedge on our right, go over two stiles in quick succession and diagonally across another field to two more stiles in the bottom corner, then down a narrow path between hedges and out into a road.

Here we turn right for Shamley Green, a village built round two triangular village greens, most of the houses being 16th and 17th century. On reaching the first green we turn right with the little pond on our left then turn right along the next green with *"The Red Lion"* on our right. We bear left across the green from *"The Red Lion"* to pass the red brick chapel on our right and go down Sweetwater Lane. In a few yards we turn right along an enclosed footpath keeping forward in the same direction along Nursery Hill and then along a residential road. At No. 42 there is an enclosed footpath on the left which soon leaves the houses and after going through a small plantation enters a field. We ignore the stile on the right and cross the field to the far corner to another stile leading to an enclosed footpath which crosses a drive and continues forward. When we reach Cherry Tree Cottage on the left we turn right down a drive and out to a road, where again we turn right. We continue along this pleasant little road for less than half a mile passing some delightful houses, and as the road turns sharply right we take a signposted footpath on the left passing some Great Dane Kennels. We keep straight ahead, crossing the mill stream and turning right with the drive past the 15th century Mill House.

We come out to the main road and turn left past St. John's Seminary, taking the higher level path parallel with the road. Just past "Stephouse" on the right we go up some steps on the right and through a gate into a field. We follow a well defined path straight across the field to go through a kissing gate, turning left down to a timbered farmhouse. We then turn left down a minor road to the main road, turning right for the centre of Wonersh, passing the 15th century Grantley Arms on our left. From the centre of the village we take the road signposted to Bramley where there are many lovely black and white timbered houses. Through a brick archway on the left is a secluded garden given by Mrs. F. H. Cook for the quiet use of the residents. Note the interesting friezes either side of the archway.

Just past the entrance to the church on our left we take a footpath on the right through a kissing gate by the side of a beautiful ancient timbered house. At the end of a brick wall we turn right through "squeeze" posts down a track to a road, passing the Memorial Hall on our left. We cross the road diagonally left and with the Health Centre on our right follow the trees and a ditch on the right to another road where we turn right. In a few yards we take the signposted footpath on our left by the timbered farmhouse we passed earlier and continue along this fenced path gradually going uphill to the top of Barnet Hill. Soon after passing the house at the top of the hill we take an enclosed footpath on our right down to a stile leading into a fenced bridleway. Here we turn right passing a small chapel and graveyard on our right and later some farm buildings on our left. At a junction of paths we turn left following the fence round on our left and continue along this path, returning to the lane we were in earlier, and out to the road. We then turn right and just past the Village Hall take the signposted bridleway on our left. The bridleway continues straight ahead, but we turn right by a house along a wide track. At the point where the tracks cross, we turn right between gorse and heath on a sandy path and when in about 50 yards two narrow paths turn off on our left we take the second one among heather finally leading back to the car parking space.

For Chilworth Station we continue down Sampleoak Lane.

Refreshments are available at Shamley Green with a choice of inns. At Wonersh the little corner shop sells ice cream.

Gomshall

**Shere Heath, Albury Park 4¾ miles
Shere Heath, Albury Heath, Blackheath, Brook. 7 miles**

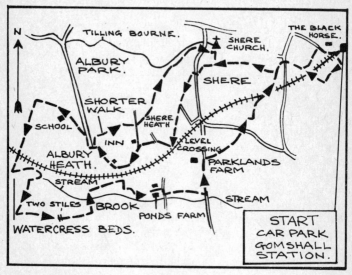

Walk 3

THIS is a heath, park and farmland walk taking us past many beautiful old houses. It is suitable for any time of the year and very little mud will be encountered in this mainly sandy area.

How to get there: By train or No. 425 and 439 bus to Gomshall Station where there is a car park.

For both walks:
   Leaving Gomshall Station down the approach road we turn

left in the main road under the railway bridge and immediately turn right along Wonham Way, a stony track. We cross a stream, pass a cottage on the left and as the drive turns sharply left we turn right through a gate along a fenced path with a large house on the right and farm buildings on the left. At the end of the path we turn right under the railway bridge and then left along a small road to a junction. We go straight across to a signposted bridleway bearing left. Opposite a house called Old Barn on the left, we turn right with another house called Highlands on the right, keeping on the right-hand path between fences with views of Netley Heath up on the right. Soon coming into open fields with a hedge on the right we keep straight ahead noticing Shere Church down on our right. Our path comes out to a small residential road along which we continue to another road at the *Shere* village sign where we cross to a signposted bridleway opposite. This leads us through a small council estate and into a fenced path which goes uphill into woods.

When the track forks we take the right-hand fork for a few yards only and then a small left hand uphill path through pine trees which later give way to oak and birch. This is Shere Heath. The path comes out to a small road which we cross to a track opposite continuing to a junction of five paths where we take the one on the right going under telegraph wires and down to level crossing gates. We turn right, away from the gates, into a wide cart track for a short distance. At a crossing track we turn left, then right on the heath keeping the hedge on our left. This path later drops down on the left to a sunken path and brings us out to the road at *The "William IVth" Inn* at Little London. We turn left down the road, taking a footpath on the right just before the railway bridge.

We go up this fenced path, through white posts and on to Albury Heath, keeping straight ahead and passing a small red brick building on the right. We continue along the sandy track to a wider crossing track with a car park on the left. Just before reaching the road we take a small path on the right amid bracken to a crossing track.

For the shorter version via Albury Park
We go over this crossing track, with houses down on the right, and quite soon at the next junction of paths take the left fork out

to a road in which we turn right. We pass some houses on the right and as the road bears right we take a footpath on the left through a gate into Albury Park and down an avenue of fine chestnut trees, keeping on the main path over a stile and then to a gate by the lodge on the right. Keeping along the track with the river and ford on our left, and passing some delightful old houses on our right, we come out to the main street and village of Shere. We cross the main street to a small road opposite leading to the church. At the end of the houses on the right and opposite the church we go through a gate and up a hedged path, at the end of which we turn left with a hedge on our left. Keeping on this path, along which we came earlier, we come to a lane in which we turn left and out to a road.

We cross this road to take the road signposted to Dorking, turning left at the railway bridge and out to the main road at Gomshall Mill. Turning right in the main road we pass *"The Black Horse"* on the left and Gomshall Station is just beyond.

For the longer version over Blackheath and Brook
At the crossing track we turn left to a road and cross straight over, turning right at the edge of a playing field parallel with the road. We cross tracks leading to a pavilion and keeping the trees on our right we take a narrow and easily missed footpath in the right-hand corner into trees. This path bears right down to a wide sandy track which leads to a white cottage on the left and we go up a small path opposite to a clearing with school buildings on the left. Notice the chimneys which are characteristic of the old buildings in this area. Passing the school buildings and a fence we go through a gate to a singposted footpath on the left. Ignoring a downward path on the right we continue forward to a crossing track with stiles each side and take the left-hand one through a plantation at the end of which is another stile into a field. Here we turn left towards two or three large trees, noticing on our right St. Martha's Church on the top of the hill.

We go down the field and across the railway, following the fence down to a lovely black and white timbered farm house. After going through two gates and between wooden farm buildings we pass watercress beds on our right and come out to a lane where we turn right into a sandy uphill path. Near the top

16

we take the first track on our left passing a large pine tree on the right. We keep left at the fork and at a crossing track go left over a stile along a wide grassy track through a plantation. Crossing two stiles close together we go downhill over a field keeping straight ahead towards a fence. At the end of the wire fence and at the footpath sign we turn slightly left to a gate and across a green to a road at Brook with a shop on the right.

We turn left in the road and over a stream then turn right into the lane to Shere and Peaslake, passing some delightful cottages, particularly Chennels built in 1636 with interesting wood carvings on the roof timbers. We keep along this little road to the railway bridge which we passed near earlier in the walk, and just before it take the signposted footpath on the right along a tarmac lane to Ponds Farm at the end. We cross the farm lane, go up some steps opposite and cross the centre of a field to trees and a road. Here we turn left and just past Parklands Farm on the left take a signposted footpath on the right between wire fences. At a wider track we turn left and out to a road where we turn right and almost immediately turn left along a signposted bridleway. Keeping straight ahead on an enclosed grassy track which bears right with a brick wall, we soon go through an iron gate and turn left across a field. Just before the hedge ahead the path forks and we take the right fork across to the corner of the field and join a bridleway crossing the railway. We continue down to a wider lane and keep straight ahead with Old Barn on the right, bearing right out to a road. Gomshall Station can be reached by crossing this road and taking the road signposted to Dorking. We turn left at the railway bridge and out to the main road at Gomshall Mill, turning right in the main road, passing the *"Black Horse"* on the left. Gomshall Station is just beyond.

Refreshments: Teas and morning coffee at Gomshall Mill. Inns at Little London, Shere and Gomshall.

Windmill Hill

**Reynards Hill, Winterfold Heath,
Helmet Copse, Dicks Hill 4½ miles**

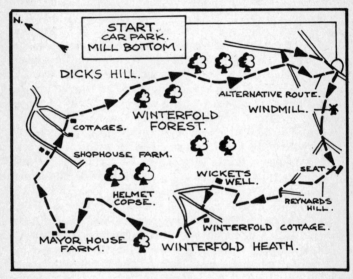

Walk 4

THIS is a walk through heather, bilberries, pines and birches on the less frequented hills west of Holmbury and Pitch Hills, with wide expansive views. Deer can frequently be seen and it is a good walk for any time of the year.

How to get there: By car to a car park at the southern end of Mill Bottom at the foot of Pitch Hill. Turn off the A.25 at Shere and the car park is four miles down on the left just before reaching *The Windmill Inn*.

Leaving the car park we cross the road to an uphill track at the side of Mill Cottage, avoiding a sunken path which bears right. Our path resembles a gully at first but when we have reached the top of Windmill Hill it leads us past a windmill, now used as a residence, on our left. Ignoring tracks leading right, and passing other buildings on our left we continue downhill and reach the road at a fork. Between the forks is a car parking space on the left and we take a footpath leading out of this space on the right. This fairly broad track leads us through woods and out to a clearing at the top of Reynards Hill where we can rest on a seat provided and admire the view. Hascombe Hill can be seen on the right in the distance. Continuing on our path, we eventually wind our way out to the road where we turn left and after about 150 yards, near a notice, *Jelleys Hollow,* on our left, we take the second of two footpaths turning off on our right. This leads us over Winterfold Heath.

After about a quarter of a mile, at a junction of paths, we turn right and in a few yards right again on a wide path which goes down a dip. At the bottom of the dip we turn left along a small path between conifers, and after about 300 yards we emerge on a main crossing track at Wickets Well, with water clearly visible although surrounded by fencing and somewhat overgrown with vegetation.

Returning to where our small path emerged on to the main crossing track facing Wickets Well we take another very small path immediately on our left which soon bears right uphill.

Our path soon flattens out and we carry on until we come out on to a wide crossing track where we turn right and immediately left, dropping to a slightly lower level. We are now at the hedge surrounding Winterfold Cottage and we turn right past the cottage continuing forward on the lane and out to the road.

We cross the road to a footpath opposite and after a few yards, at a junction of paths, we keep left and cross a wider track. After 100 yards or so, just before a sunken crossing track, we go over a signposted stile on our right and forward along a pleasant, wide, grassy "ride" with a conifer plantation known as Helmet Copse on our right, and keeping parallel with the sunken track down on our left. When the grassy ride turns right we go forward over a stile on the right of a gate, under trees for a short distance, still keeping parallel with the sunken track. We turn left through posts into a wider track, almost immediately crossing the sunken track and keeping ahead for Mayorhouse Farm.

Just before the farmhouse itself we take a cart track on the right passing between farm buildings and noticing white doves around the barn on the left. At the end of the buildings we go through a gate to a field footpath which leads along the lowest level of the field, under telegraph wires, to a stile and then keeping in the same direction to another stile in the corner of the field. We drop down into an enclosed lane which we cross, going up the bank and over two stiles in quick succession, crossing the field to another two stiles in wattle fencing, another field, another stile, then a fenced path, over two more stiles, along the edge of a cottage garden, two more stiles and finally out to the road at Shophouse Farm. Eleven stiles in a quarter of a mile!

We turn left in the road and almost immediately right, along a signposted fenced footpath, then over a stile and across a wide drive to another stile opposite, keeping straight ahead, passing a cottage named Pooh Corner. We go down some wooden steps and through a woodland path, over a ditch and bear left up to a grassy track with a cottage on the opposite side.

Here we turn left over a culvert and immediately right, with a telegraph pole on our left, into a path which we follow for over a mile, first with a stream and Dick's Hill on our left and later with the stream on our right. In dry weather the stream is practically non-existent and in wet weather it is inclined to overflow on to the footpath in places. Proceeding along our path, at the first fork we take the right, higher path and at a later fork we keep right again. We eventually come out on a wide crossing track which we cross to another wide track going uphill. We ignore a path on the left and keep uphill until the path ends at a gate. *Here we turn left to a road which we cross to a horse track among the trees opposite and go forward bearing right with the track. Other tracks join ours from the left but we continue bearing right and going gradually uphill. At the highest part, among open pine trees, our path branches to the left but disregarding this we keep forward a few more yards to a junction of several paths. Here we turn sharply left on a smaller path bearing right and downhill, passing an old car dump on our left, and are soon out to the road by Mill Cottage opposite the car park.

*   Alternative end involving nearly half a mile of walking on pleasant roads: Here we turn left to a road, then left again for a few yards to another road, where we turn right. We are now less than half a mile from the car park and to avoid the road we can walk among the trees on the left, keeping parallel with the road. At a road junction we continue forward on the road signposted to Ewhurst and Cranleigh and are soon back at the car park.

Peaslake

Holmbury Hill and Pitch Hill
5 miles

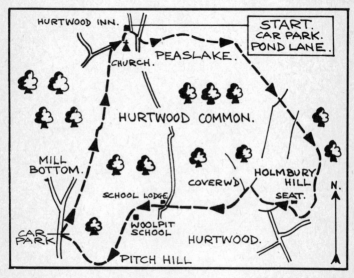

Walk 5

THIS walk takes us through woods, gorse and heather to Leith Hill's more southerly neighbour and the wide top of Pitch Hill. From excavations in 1930 proof was obtained of a hill camp on Holmbury Hill dating from 150 B.C. to 50 A.D. The camp is now rather overgrown with brambles and bracken but can be traced round the four sides of the top. This is a wonderful walk for any time of the year, but in winter the views are enhanced by the absence of leaves and undergrowth.

How to get there: By train or 425 or 439 bus to Gomshall then a 448 bus to Peaslake (Mon-Sat). By car to Peaslake turning off the A.25 at Gomshall. The car park is down Pond Lane next to *The Hurtwood Inn*.

Walking back to the Inn we turn left, then right, then left again up Radnor Road opposite the War Memorial. Almost immediately there is a steep footpath on the left but if this looks too steep we can continue along the road and turn left along Plaws Hill which will bring us to the top of the steep footpath.

With Tor Cottage on our left we go forward on a well defined path under trees, over various crossing tracks, down a dip and up the other side, soon bearing slightly right with a field on our left. At a fork we keep left with fields around a large house still on our left. Just past the house the path bears slightly right taking us into the woods to a stile. We go over the stile and a crossing track to a track opposite. In a few yards we turn right at another crossing track keeping on through the conifers and soon going uphill, after ignoring a track forking off on our right.

Our track is now very sandy and the vegetation mainly conifers, heather and bracken. After half a mile a small path forks on our right and we can now see our track ahead dipping down to a valley and up the other side. We cross the valley and on the other side go over a crossing track at the top of the hill and continue forward on a small path. We are soon at a junction of paths at a small green "triangle" and continue on, maintaining direction. Our path then bears slightly right and downhill to a junction of five paths. We take the third on the left, which is straight ahead, and as the path bears right again and forks we take the right fork.

The hillside is now fairly open giving good views on our left. At the next fork we go right and later at a T junction we turn right on to a more main path leading uphill. Almost at once it forks and we take the left fork and continue up to the open space and circular memorial seat at the top of Holmbury Hill.

Leaving the memorial on our left we cross the open space to two paths. We take the left one, leading slightly downwards and continue round the edge of the hill, ignoring three paths which successively join us on our right. The path then bears right and at a T junction we turn left on to a main path and immediately take the right fork going downhill on a wide path to a line of concrete blocks preventing car access where we turn left along a broad track, bearing left to an open space on our right. We

23

follow down to a narrow tarmac road where we turn right and after a few yards take a path on the left through trees, going slightly downhill.

We turn left again on a path at the bottom and soon cross a stile on our right. A second stile leads us to an enclosed path, marked *Footpath to Pitch Hill,* which takes us across the valley giving pleasant views. When the path goes slightly uphill to a holly thicket we continue forward and are finally out on the road. We are now opposite the lodge of The Woolpit School and the public footpath goes through the school grounds. We take the drive into the school leaving the lodge on our right and when the drive turns left towards the main school building we take a smaller path on the right and proceed uphill on a grassy path under trees, leaving the sports field on our right. We do not bear left behind the school but continue up through a gap in the perimeter fencing. Our path bears left and uphill and we emerge on to a well defined track where we turn left, shortly encountering a fork where we turn right through bilberries, birch, bracken and conifers. At the next cross track we turn left and eventually emerge into the open with panoramic views and the South Downs visible on a clear day. We continue on our path, keeping to the left on the edge of the hill top and finally come to the main open space of Coneyhurst, or Pitch Hill with O.S. trig point at a height of 843ft. We continue beyond the trig point on a sandy track, going right at a fork, and soon left around fencing encircling a disused quarry. We can bear right around the quarry dropping down on various paths to the road, or continue on our path leaving the quarry on our right. In both cases we reach the road by a car parking space.

Without actually going out to the road we turn right through the car parking area and along the track known as Mill Bottom under the trees which are mainly beech. At a fork we keep left and continue on a pleasant and easy path in the same direction for over a mile until we reach an open space which leads out to the road. Here we turn right and using a parallel path at a slightly higher level on the right of the road, continue into Peaslake passing the church and a small shop where ice cream and cups of tea are sold. The *Hurtwood Inn* is on our left and the car park behind it.

Refreshments: Peaslake.

Westcott

**Broomy Down, Townhurst Wood,
The Rookery. 6¾ miles**

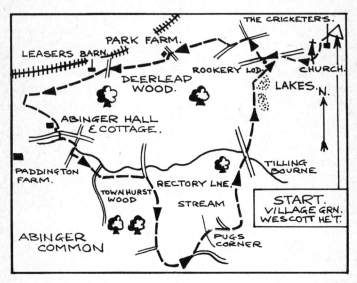

Walk 6

THIS is an interesting walk over heathland and through woodland where deer abound. It affords delightful views across the valley and is pleasant at any time of the year. Very little mud will be encountered.

How to get there: There is a reasonably good bus service Nos. 412, 425 or 439 from Dorking to Westcott which is about 2 miles from the centre of Dorking. Cars can be parked in the side road leading from *The Cricketers* up to Westcott Church.

From the triangular village green at Westcott we continue along the main road for a few yards to *The Cricketers* where we turn left. Just past the church and opposite the graveyard on the left we take a wide path on the right leading us over a grass area in front of a few houses. We cross a small road leading to the houses and go forward on a wide track which at once forks. We take the left fork, slightly downhill, keeping to the main path and ignoring branching paths. Our path becomes gully-like with orange coloured sandhills on the right and we are soon out to the main road by the Rookery Lodge.

We cross the main road turning left, continue past Balchins Lane and turn right up Coast Hill Lane, which almost immediately turns left while we continue forward on an enclosed footpath between gardens. We are soon walking between wire fences in an area of holly, beech and conifer trees and after bearing left and slightly downhill we are out on a small tarmac drive. Here we turn left on to a farm track bounded by fields keeping right when it forks after a short distance. After about 100 yards we turn right at a T junction and proceed through trees on a wide track. Ignoring a smaller left track through trees we keep to the main track which leads towards a red brick house which we pass, continuing on a field path to Park Farm.

With the farm house on the right we go through a gate with farm buildings either side. We keep on this track with Deerleap Woods on the left and open fields on the right with pleasant views across the valley to White Downs. After about half a mile we are out in the road which leads from Effingham to the A.25. We turn left and then almost immediately right on a well defined path passing the Bishop Wilberforce monument, which marks the spot where he was thrown from his horse and killed in 1873, and Leasers Barn. After a while we cross a stile leading to an open field and bear left up to another stile leading into woodland. We go forward and uphill on a wide track for about 150 yards when we turn left on another wide track. Soon we have a clearing on our right at the end of which we turn left on a crossing track and down through pine trees to an open field ahead which we reach by going over an unusual stile. We go forward and slightly left over this field leaving some isolated trees on our left then through a gate along a path with the walled courtyard of the stable block of Abinger Hall on our right. This pathway has been planted with bulbs for the enjoyment of walkers and near the cottage on the right some unusual toothwort may be seen growing at the base of the trees in spring. A business dealing with minerals, rocks, geological specimens, etc. is carried on here and genuine enquirers are welcome to call at the cottage.

Our path comes out to the main road which we cross to a stile opposite and going diagonally across the field to a holly tree and stile we come out to a secondary road where we turn right and then shortly left into a smaller road. We pass Abinger Mill House on the left and go through a gate taking a path into a wood with a stream on our left. We remain on this path through Townhurst Wood for over half a mile. Deer may be seen here if we are quiet. We continue over a stile into a road, Rectory Lane, where we turn right. We remain on this road for almost half a mile and about 150 yards past a turning on the right and just past some wooden gate posts at the side of the road we take a footpath on our left keeping left when it forks and continuing forward over a crossing track. Our path bears left and is soon parallel with a small road on our right. At Mundies Farm track we join the road and then turn left down a private drive to Pugs Corner. The drive ends at a house where we turn right crossing a stream by a bridge and going over wooden bars to a small path opposite going steeply uphill. When the path flattens out we have a wire fence on our left and open woods on our right. After a short distance we go over a stile into a wider track and almost immediately turn left and soon left again, still with the wire fence on our left. We continue along this beautiful grassy track and just before a five-barred gate across the track we turn right down a well defined path which soon goes downhill, bears left and becomes parallel with a sunken road on our right.

We eventually come out over a stile to the road, where we turn left, and after crossing the Tillingbourne, in a few yards we turn right, opposite a wooden gate on the left, going uphill into trees and emerging into a private drive. The public footpath crosses the drive diagonally left up a steep bank, weaving through the trees to a bridleway where we turn left to a house. This path is very obscure and in practice it is easier to turn left along the private drive to a house.

We pass the house on our left, going through brick gate posts

27

and turning right on a footpath to the left of a bridleway. At the end of the path we turn right, cross a wide track immediately turning left through wooden posts on an enclosed path which takes us steeply downhill to a wider bridleway where we maintain direction passing a lake on our right and going through the Rookery on the main drive past several delightful houses. We finally join the main road with the Rookery Lodge on our left. We turn right and take the footpath parallel with the road past the sandhills on our left. We keep forward on the main path crossing a drive and the open space in front of houses and finally out to the road by the graveyard where we turn left down the road to Westcott Church.

Friday Street

**Abinger Bottom, High Ashes,
Holmbury St. Mary,
Pasture Wood and back to Friday Street.
5½ miles circular walk from
the Friday Street Car Park
but if done from Wotton Hatch Hotel
it adds another 2½ miles,
making 8 miles in all**

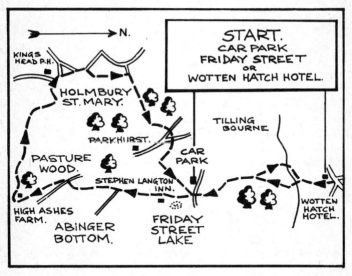

Walk 7

THIS is a woodland walk for any time of the year, with bluebells and foxgloves in season and deer to be seen by the observant who keep quiet. There is very little mud even in winter and plenty of shade for a hot summer's day when it is advisable to take the hilly part of Pasture Wood at a very gentle pace. It is particularly beautiful on a sunny winter's day when the views are not obscured by trees in full leaf.

How to get there: By car to Friday Street. The car park is 200 yards west on the Abinger Road. Bus Nos. 412,425 or 439 to Wotton Hatch.

Starting from the Friday Street Car Park
With the car park behind us and facing the road we turn right on to a narrow path parallel with the road, but at a higher level, following it to some wooden steps, which we go down turning left into the road and right to Friday Street lake.

From Wotton Hatch Hotel to Friday Street (just under $1\frac{1}{4}$ miles)
Leaving the hotel on our right we take the drive to a gate at the side of a wooden school building (yellow waymark), over a stile and diagonally right across a field to the corner. (N.B. *not* over a stile in the fence on the right.) Continue over another stile, (yellow waymark), down through a strip of woodland and over a meadow crossing the Tillingbourne. Our path then takes us up towards a wood and over a stile, bearing right uphill through woods, crossing a wider track and keeping in the same direction uphill with a wire fence on the right, then downhill to ponds and a stream in the valley. We turn left at the T junction and go along this track for about half a mile, then over a stile by a bridge and pond on the right, keeping straight ahead on the wide bridleway, passing a couple of cottages, and out to the lake at Friday Street.

With the lake on our left we walk along the little road passing *The Stephen Langton Inn* and at the end of the lane we keep straight ahead on a narrow footpath for about half a mile when it joins a tarmac lane. We turn left into Abinger Bottom and as the lane turns left we keep straight ahead on a path through open woods. When a fence appears on the left at a crossing track we turn right uphill to a small road where we turn left. Almost immediately there is a signposted path on the right through trees to the corner of a field ahead and a gate post, the gate itself having long since gone. We do not go through the

30

gateway but turn left parallel to the road with the field on our right, keeping just inside the wood with beech trees on the right. At the fork we keep right and near High Ashes farm buildings on our right the path bears slightly right to join a farm drive. We turn right in the drive passing the farm on our right and as the drive bears right into the farm we take the left downhill path inside the wood with a field on the right. Keeping straight ahead we ignore all side tracks. On a clear day there are some very good views of the South Downs on the left. After nearly a mile we have a broken chestnut paling fence on our left and we continue downhill to a road.

We turn left at the road and down to the main road and Holmbury St. Mary, where we turn right. For refreshment *The King's Head Inn* is along the first turning on the left.

To continue the walk we keep straight along the main road passing a bus shelter on the right and at an old village pump we turn right on a gravel drive, through a gate and straight ahead. At the fork just past the lodge we keep left, then straight on. At the next fork we keep right on the main track, soon with a wire fence on the left, crossing a track with a house and pond on the left. Keeping forward we pass a brick hut on the right and pond on the left, to go through some posts with a swimming pool on the left. Just before a gate we take the stile on the right with a yellow waymark on a tree, and go steeply uphill through Pasture Woods. At the top the path levels out giving fine open views of White Downs on the left. Keeping straight on and ignoring crossing tracks we go through open woods with isolated scots pines, down a dip in more open country, then up into a wood and finally down to a field ahead and over a stile by a holly bush. We are now on an enclosed path which bears left out to a road. We cross straight over to a gravel path and are soon out to another road.

Here we turn right and after a few yards take a narrow path on the left into woods. When the path forks after a few yards we keep left and continue along this narrow path over several crossing tracks coming to a wide sandy crossing track with a large sandy mound on the right. We cross this sandy track to a small path opposite, bearing right. This path comes to a junction of several paths and we take the first on the left which soon becomes a sunken path through heather and bracken, taking us under some telegraph wires and out to a road.

For the car park we go up the wooden steps on the left and along the path which follows the road at a higher level.

If we are making for Wotton Hatch Hotel we turn right at the road to Friday Street lake and turn left into the bridleway along which we came. We keep along this for just over half a mile but instead of turning right on the path we used at the beginning of the walk we keep straight on. The track goes downhill and bears right to some crossing tracks which we cross continuing down with open fields on either side of the trees. We go over a stile and stream, then up a field ahead to a stile by the hedge. We turn right in the drive, continue under an iron girder which spans the drive, over the stile in the fence on our right and across the meadow back to Wotton Hatch Hotel.

Refreshments: Holmbury St. Mary.

Horsley

Sheepleas 5 miles

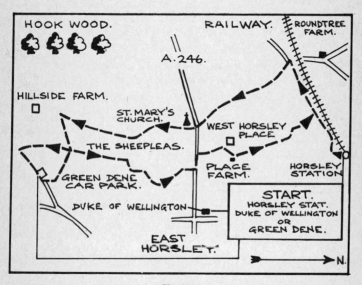

Walk 8

THIS is a pleasant walk at any time but makes a perfect autumn walk in country which compares with Burnham Beeches in Buckinghamshire for colour, the yellowing larches and dark green pines complementing the beech trees.

How to get there: By train to Horsley Station. By No. 408 Green bus to *The Duke of Wellington,* East Horsley. By car on the A.246 from Dorking to Guildford turning left on the signposted road to Green Dene and Sheepleas half a mile east of East Horsley, continuing down the lane for one and a half miles to the car park on the right.

33

If using 408 bus to the Duke of Wellington

Walk towards Guildford for about quarter of a mile and take the bridleway on the right to Place Farm and continue the walk from (A).

If starting from Horsley Station

We turn right down the approach road, crossing the main road to take the small road by the side of Horsley Hotel, keeping parallel with the railway on our right. This soon becomes a footpath alongside the railway and eventually comes out into a road. Now continue the walk from (B).

Walks 8 and 9 form a figure of eight and if a 10 mile walk is desired instead of turning left for the car park we cross the road to the signposted bridleway into Mountain Wood and follow Walk 9.

Starting from the car park

We take a path at the right-hand corner of the car park to a wire fence and turn right, turning left at a crossing track and going uphill. Sheepleas is riddled with paths so we must take care. Ignoring the next turning on the right we come to a fork where we keep right, and going slightly uphill cross an avenue of yew trees, and after about 200 yards we come out to an open space by a signpost. We turn right to another signpost and turn right again, soon coming into an open space across which we walk to a crossing track and turn left into beech trees. Under these we turn sharply right. The path is not very distinct as it is covered with beech leaves. Keeping along this path for some distance to a junction of several tracks, we turn right into a woodland track with fields on our left and right. St. Mary's Church, West Horsley, is soon visible in the distant trees on our left. When we come to the road we turn left and soon take a bridleway on the right to Place Farm.

(A)   We follow the footpath signs through the farm into a grassy track, at first hedged and then across open fields and eventually coming to the railway line. For return to the station turn right.

(B)   We turn left and follow the path alongside the railway line until it comes out into a road where we turn left and in a few yards, just past the 40 m.p.h. sign, we go over a stile in the hedge on our left. Keeping the hedge on our left we cross the field to another stile and turn slightly diagonally right across the next large field to a gap in the hedge, over a stile and, with the hedge on our left, come out opposite St. Mary's Church, West Horsley. Crossing the main road we take the bridleway with the church on our right.

This church is well worth a visit and much of it is very old. There is a fragment of Saxon stonework and late Norman pillars and arches; the tower doorway is also late Norman. A 12th century wall painting depicts St. Christopher, the patron saint of travellers, and pilgrims' crosses can be seen on the arch of the 12th century north doorway.

When the bridleway enters woods we keep right through wooden fence posts following the main track through the wood, then on a slightly uphill path, and finally, in just over half a mile, out to an open space. Maintaining direction we cross the open space with seats on our left and re-enter the woods again.

Very soon a house and an open field become visible ahead on our left and we turn left with the open field on our right through the trees. As our path approaches the corner of the field we turn left again, still inside the wood, along the edge of a field until we join a crossing track, where there is a seat. We turn sharply right down a path, fenced at first, and finally out to the road.

Turning left in the road we are soon at the car park.

Refreshments: The Duke of Wellington *turning right at the main road*.

Mountain Wood

**and Netley Heath 5 miles.
A circular walk from the car park
in Green Dene through woodland**

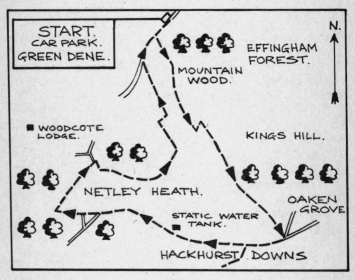

Walk 9

THIS is a lovely walk for all seasons but is particularly recommended for the autumn when the larches of Mountain Wood are yellowing. In addition there are many different types of fungi to be seen and blackberries and sweet chestnuts for the gathering.

How to get there: By car on the A.246 Leatherhead to Guildford, turning left on the signposted road to Green Dene and

Sheepleas half a mile east of East Horsley, continuing down the lane for a mile and a half to the car park on the right.

From the car park we turn right along the road for a short distance to a signposted bridleway on the left into Mountain Wood. We keep on the main track going uphill at first and later ignoring a left fork. After about a mile we pass on our right a very knobbly beech tree and then have a wire fence on our left for a short distance before turning right into a conifer plantation. At the end of the conifers we turn left with larch trees on our right and pines on our left. Later we have an open aspect on our left and then drop steeply down to a wide forestry track. We turn left for some 200 yards turning right through a clearing on a path for nearly a mile, first under trees and later becoming open. Ignoring a left fork we finally come to a droveway where we turn right, after about a quarter of a mile turning left through posts to the open space of Hackhurst Downs, keeping forward on the main path to the top of the ridge with views down into Gomshall and Holmbury Hill straight ahead. Having admired the view, we retrace our steps back to the main droveway and turn left, later passing a static water tank on the right. We keep on the droveway over Netley Heath for a good mile and when it turns sharply left we take a smaller path straight ahead leading us into a wider track. After about 50 yards, just after a track turns off on the left, we take a path on our right down through trees and out to a tarmac drive which we cross to a small path opposite, keeping on this for about a quarter of a mile.

When the path forks we keep right to a clump of fir trees behind which we turn sharply right through wooden posts on a small path leading down to a tarmac drive. Here we turn right and then shortly left, still on a tarmac drive. At a crossing drive we turn right and as this turns right and uphill we take a small path on the left in the valley soon with a wire fence on our left.

At the end of the wire fence we turn left steeply uphill and continue on this path over a crossing track in the woods to another crossing track and into the open. Here we turn right and then left with pines on our right, later turning right with the pines and keeping straight ahead along the main path, now quite narrow, through trees and out into the road. Here we turn right and go along the road for a short distance to the car park on our left.

Ranmore

**Six Acre Copse, High Barn,
Yewtree Farm, Pigdon. 4½ miles**

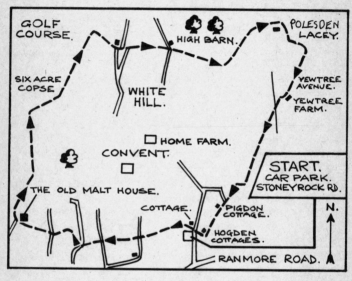

Walk 10

THIS is a varied walk of woods and fields in a little known area, with changing views. It is lovely in spring and autumn while the bare trees of winter open up the viewpoints still further although it may be somewhat muddy in wet weather.

How to get there: 412 bus from **Dorking** to **Stoney Rock Road** runs Monday — Friday only.

By car on the A.24 from London turning off for Guildford just before Dorking Station (Ashcombe Road) but keeping straight on along the Ranmore Road instead of turning left for Guildford. Stoneyrock Road is the second turning on the right about 3 miles from Dorking Station, and there is a car park on the left just before a cottage.

Starting from the car park near the cottage with two pine trees in the garden and keeping the cottage on our right we go straight ahead for a short distance to an enclosed path with fields on both sides. The path, which is rather muddy during wet weather, goes down a dip with a house on the left, then up a drive to a road.

We cross the road to a gravelled drive ahead and as this bears right we cross a stile, maintaining our direction, then go over another stile and *straight* down the field. There is a left diagonal path but we avoid this. We arrive at a kissing gate leading into a road. Crossing the road to a footpath almost opposite, slightly to the right, we go up through a wood with fields on the right, over a couple of stiles and at the second stile bear right to another stile and footpath signs. We turn left with a wire fence on our left to a gate into a wide bridleway.

Here we turn right and very soon left over a signposted stile across a field, then through a wood to a beautiful timbered house, *The Old Malt House,* which we keep on our right, turning right into a bridleway. We follow the bridleway for about a quarter of a mile and just before the next house on the left we turn right on a very small path. After about 300 yards we take an even smaller path forking off on the left through the woods, Six Acre Copse, and bringing us eventually out to the edge of a field. We walk along the edge of the field with woods on our left to the corner of the field and then re-enter the woods keeping on a well defined path and finally coming out to a golf course.

Maintaining our direction, we cross the golf course to a clump of trees where we turn right at a signpost. With the electricity building on our right we go straight ahead across another golf green to a grassy track with the grounds of a large house on our left, coming out to a road. Crossing the road we take a track opposite which leads us to another road and High Barn.

We go through the posts opposite and continue on a path through woods to a junction of paths and a field. We skirt this large field with the woods on our left finally reaching a horse trough and a crossing track where we turn right. When this bears right we turn left over a gate into a field, turning left along the top of the field with lovely views across the valley. At the end we go through a gate.

After going through the gate we turn immediately right down a spectacular avenue of yew trees and when it joins another track we bear right passing Yew Tree Farm on our left and ignoring a path forking off to the right.

Soon after passing the farm we turn right into a field through a gate at the side of a large beech tree. We keep along the top edge of this field with the woods on our left and lovely views across the valley over to High Barn. At the end of the first field, after going through the remains of a hedge with a few isolated large trees, we bear diagonally right down a sloping field to a stile in a hedge which we cross bringing us into a wide cart track bounded by a flint wall.

Here we turn left and go straight ahead passing Pigdon on our right. At the next building, Hogden Cottages, we turn right uphill with the cottage gardens on our right and finally out to the road and the cottage with its two pines and the car park.

Ranmore and Polesden Lacey

**From Boxhill Station through the woods of Ranmore
and Polesden Lacey 6½ miles**

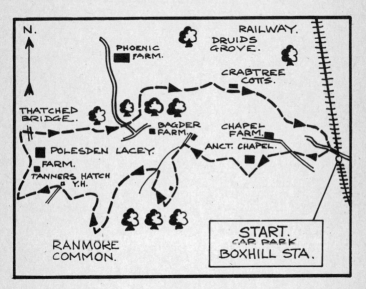

N.

RAILWAY.
DRUIDS GROVE.
PHOENIC FARM.
CRABTREE COTTS.
THATCHED BRIDGE.
BAGDER FARM.
CHAPEL FARM.
ANCT. CHAPEL.
POLESDEN LACEY.
FARM.
TANNERS HATCH Y.H.
RANMORE COMMON.
START.
CAR PARK
BOXHILL STA.

Walk 11

A ZIGZAG walk in the lovely woods of Ranmore Common with beech and oak trees, bluebells, foxgloves, orchids, and deer if you are quiet. It is recommended for any time of the year.

How to get there: By train to Boxhill Station. There is a car park at the station. Green bus 470 or Green Line Coaches 712, 713 or 714 to Burford Bridge Hotel where there is a free car park.

Leaving Boxhill Station we go up the steps and turn left over the bridge taking the left fork, Chapel Lane. We stay on the

road for half a mile but there is a parallel footpath on the left for
some of the way. Passing Burney Road and the last of the
houses on our left, we take a footpath diagonally left between
wire fences across a field to a T junction where we turn left. The
remains of an ancient chapel can be seen on the right. We continue along this tree fringed bridleway and just underneath the
pylon lines we take a right fork and after a few yards we go over
a stile on the right, keeping parallel with the telegraph wires to
another stile by two water tanks. Keeping along this path with a
wire fence and open fields on our right and a sloping wood on
the left, we go over another stile and along a hedge on our right
to a cottage and a road. Here we turn left and after a quarter of
a mile we pass a cottage on the right, then an open field, soon
coming to a wood on our right. Just inside the wood we go
through a gate on the right with a blue waymark on a tree and
go uphill. At the top of the hill at a T junction and a blue
waymark on a beech tree we turn right going slightly downhill.
At the end of the wood the path turns left down a waymarked
path between wire fences to a bridleway at the bottom.

We turn left across the field and just inside the wood we take
the left fork through a wire gate continuing through the valley of
a forestry plantation to a junction of paths and a big beech tree.
Here we turn right, doubling back at a higher level than our
previous path. Watch out on the right for a post at a corner of a
wired enclosure just past a yew tree and turn left straight up
through open trees. There is no path but by bearing very slightly
left going uphill we come to a larch plantation through which
there is a cleared track which comes out to a wide bridleway.
Here we turn right and almost immediately left on another wide
bridleway downhill to Tanners Hatch Youth Hostel.

We turn left and just past the hostel grounds we go over a
stile at a right fork with a wire fence on our right. The wood
gives way to open fields on the right beyond which Polesden
Lacey can be seen. We follow this path uphill through woods
again and when the fence ends, keep forward to a bridleway and
cottage where we turn right downhill, passing Polesden Farm
buildings at the bottom, then uphill again along a tarmac drive.
At the top we turn right with the drive, soon going under a small
thatched bridge, and again turning right with the drive. We pass
the entrance to Polesden Lacey on our right, the gardens of

which are well worth a visit: admission for non-members of The National Trust 15p.

To continue the walk we follow the drive for another quarter of a mile and after going slightly uphill to a line of trees on our right we turn right on a bridleway which we follow for about three quarters of a mile. Finally our bridleway turns right into woods (a minor track continues on) and soon bears left downhill. As we approach a bridge carrying a drive over the bridleway we bear right on a small uphill path taking us into the drive where we turn left over the bridge. Just beyond, as the drive bears right, we turn left into trees and bear right with a hollow on our right. This is a rather indistinct path through open beech trees but we keep the dense larch plantation on our right and watch for wooden fencing visible on the left. Making for this fencing, which is on the other side of a small road we cross the road to a path immediately opposite and follow this for about quarter of a mile to a junction of tracks and a seat. Here we turn left uphill and at a crossing track with a Norbury Park sign on the left we turn right through yew trees, and soon we have an open field on the left, then on the right giving us views of Ranmore Church, then open on the left again and we are out to Crabtree Cottages and a lane. We turn right down the lane for about a mile to Boxhill Station.

Refreshments: Polesden Lacey Tea Rooms in the summer and the kiosk at Boxhill Station on Sundays.

Dorking

Deepdene, Betchworth Golf Course, Glory Wood. 6 miles

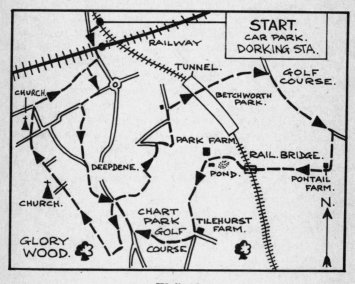

Walk 12

THIS is a pleasant walk in woods and over farmland keeping quite close to Dorking but giving us views of the hills we have walked in other walks in this book. A little mud will be encountered in winter but in April and May the larch woods near the Betchworth Golf Course are turning green and there are bluebells in the woods.

How to get there: By train or bus to Dorking Station where there is a car park.

From Dorking Station approach road we turn left into the

main road and after going under the railway bridge we take the first turning on the right. After a few yards we turn left through a wooden gate on to the drive which encircles Dorking Town Hall and follow it out to the main road, passing some tennis courts on our left. In the main road we turn right, cross to the other side, pass The Dorking Halls and take the first turning on our left, Moores Road. This soon forks and we keep right, going uphill to the open green of Cotmandene and proceed forward towards four lime trees on the green and then down towards the road ahead, where we continue in the same direction along Chart Lane.

This joins the main road which we cross bearing slightly left to a signposted footpath leading up to Deepdene. We are soon walking parallel with the main road among rhododendron thickets. We ignore a right fork and our path turns sharply left and still uphill with occasional wooden steps in the steepest parts. Keeping to the main path and disregarding branching paths we are soon at the top and as we proceed along the now flat path there are good views to be had on the right over the golf course and beyond.

Soon our path leads us to a tarmac drive where we turn left downhill bearing right between houses and gardens of the Deepdene estate. We turn right at a T junction, finally bearing right and out to a road, Punchbowl Lane, where we turn left. After just over 100 yards we turn right along a tarmac drive and in a few yards leave the drive by a footpath on the left under larch trees.

Here we may take an optional but rewarding diversion:

When a wooden fence on the left of our path comes in sight we take a small footpath slightly uphill into the trees on our right. This footpath starts clearly but is sometimes difficult to follow, but if we keep forward with the open space of the golf course on our right our footpath soon crosses a fairly open stretch of bracken giving good views of the Betchworth Clump ahead. This path eventually bears left and rejoins the original well defined path.

We continue forward soon passing on our right the club house of the Betchworth Golf Course and come out on a drive where we turn right through a white gate on to a track across the golf course. After about half a mile we turn right on a signposted footpath with a pond on our right, keeping to the edge of a field with hedge and ditchlike stream on our right and making for Pondtail Farm. A stile brings us on to the farm track which we cross to wooden bars opposite, which take us into a field, where after a few yards we turn right over a plank bridge and stile, going forward along the edge of a field with a small stream on our right. After bordering two fields we go over a broken-down stile into a narrow belt of young conifers, immediately over another stile, then turn right over wooden bars and left again on a track at the edge of a field with a ditch on our left.

After about a quarter of a mile we go under a railway bridge and across a field on a wide grassy track leading towards Park Farm. The track takes us through a wooden gate with pond and farm buildings on our left and the main farmhouse uphill on the right. We do not go over the cattle grid but turn left on another track with trees on our right and fields on our left. We proceed past a cottage on our right and downhill to a road where we turn left.

When Tilehurst Lane turns off on our left we turn right on a grassy track which leads across the golf course, uphill through woods and finally out to the main road, where we turn right. After about 150 yards and just before Chart Lane turns off we cross to the other side of the road and take a small doubling back pathway between hedges. We soon have fields on our right and on our left, screened by trees, a deep drop down to the main road. Our path bears right into open woodland known as Glory Woods, and uphill under some spectacular beech trees giving a good view of Dorking on our right.

At the end of the open space on our right our path re-enters the woods and when it shortly forks we keep left and are soon at a seat where we turn right along the main track through Glory Woods. We continue downhill and out through a gate into a field with a seat on our left and fenced woods on our right.

When we come out through school buildings to a road we go forward with a flintstone wall on our left, then down some steps, cross a road leading to a car park and downhill at the side of shops, Chequers Yard, and out into the main street of Dorking.

Here we turn right, cross over, and at the Employment Office sign turn left through the churchyard, bearing right, and out to a small road. We turn left past *The Evening Star* and turn right into a park following the Pipp Brook out to a road where we turn left down to the main road. We turn left and go under the railway bridge and so back to Dorking Station.

Refreshments: In Dorking. Tea shops and inns.

Leith Hill

**The eastern slopes of Leith Hill,
Redlands, Anstiebury Farm,
Kitlands. 5½ miles**

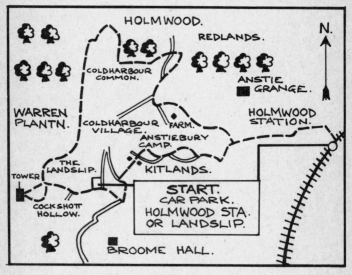

Walk 13

THIS is an exhilarating walk with magnificent views on paths amid deer country, far from the throng of people. Concentration is necessary as we twist and turn among the heather and trees.

How to get there: By car from Dorking on the Coldharbour Road to a car park at the Landslip just south of Coldharbour village and just beyond the bend sign in the road. By bus or train to Holmwood Station.

The walk starts from the car park at the Landslip but if starting from Holmwood Station turn to (3).

From the car park between the road on the left and a high slope on the right we go up a clear path which narrows as it clings to the steep hillside. At a hollow on the left we join a well defined path coming up from the road and turn right and uphill through conifers which later give way to beech trees. At the top, by a National Trust sign, *Mosses Wood,* on the right, we go through two wooden posts slightly downhill through a wood on a main track which is joined by another from the right and proceeds to a crossing track with a deep gully on our left known as Cockshott Hollow. The main path straight ahead goes up to the Tower at the top of Leith Hill but a more interesting path is the small one on the left following the edge of Cockshott Hollow and round the edge of the hill. This eventually joins the top of the main path.

The top of Leith Hill is 965 ft. but a height of 1000 ft. can be attained from the tower which was originally built by Richard Hull of Leith Hill Place in 1766. He died in 1772 and by his wish was buried in the Tower. The tower fell into decay but was restored in 1795 and the lower part filled with rubble. At some later period a turret was added giving access to the roof. It is said that thirteen counties may be seen from the top on a very clear day.

Refreshments are available most weekends and fine days during the year from a little thatched kiosk just beyond the Tower.

We retrace our steps back to the top of Cockshott Hollow and cross over to the path with the National Trust sign, *Dukes Warren.* At a crossing track we turn left. This path loops back to the path we have just left but gives superior views. Rejoining the main path we turn left and in less than 100 yards where two paths turn off on the left we take the second left one with larch trees on the left.

We pass one crossing track and at the next we turn right on a wide sandy track. In about 200 yards or so it joins a number of paths with a National Trust sign *Dukes Warren.* We take the second on the left, a small uphill path through trees and after about 150 yards go through a cutting in a small bank at a junction of paths. Keeping straight ahead on this wide forestry track we eventually come out into a broad sandy track by a static water tank.

The walk can be shortened here by turning right along the wide track for nearly half a mile until it comes out at Coldharbour village where we turn right for just over half a mile to the car park, or if Holmwood Station is required we turn left to the road junction and continue at (1).

To continue the walk from the static water tank we turn left and shortly take a well defined track downhill on the right with views of Betchworth Clump on the horizon. Crossing a very wide forestry road we go down the opposite path to Lower Merriden Farm on the left. We turn right along a wide track pass a turning on the left and take the next well defined track on the left across a field making straight for the trees opposite. Our path crosses a small stream before we take the steep uphill path ahead through conifers. At the top the path narrows and we go through heather to a wide grassy forestry track ahead and are soon out to a road.

Crossing to a gate opposite into Redlands we take the small path straight ahead uphill with conifers and a water tank on the left. At a direction stone at the top we turn right along a path with wide open views and eventually come out to a road where we turn left. At the road junction the walk can be shortened by keeping straight ahead through Coldharbour village and back to the car park. There is an inn, and confectionery and ice cream can be obtained in the village.

If Holmwood Station is required rejoin the walk here.

(1)   At the road junction we take the road signposted to Ockley and after a few yards turn left along the fenced path to Anstiebury Farm. Just beyond the farm buildings we take a stile on the right and go across a field to the far corner where there is another stile leading into woods. The path goes downhill, soon with a wire fence on our left, down to another stile and out into a field. We take a clear path across this field to a hedge and another stile, then keep along the hedge on our left and over a final stile into a lane.

For Holmwood Station we turn left and continue back the way we came, going through the kissing gate into the enclosed path which brings us back to the road and bus stop.

To continue the walk back to the Landslip, after crossing the stile into the lane we turn right and follow the lane until it comes out to a road in which we turn right passing the lodge of Kitlands on the left.

(2)   Just before a house on the right we go over the fence by a holly tree. There should be a stile but it is broken. Passing under telegraph wires, we keep along the edge of a field with the hedge on the right, over another stile and out to a lane where we turn right. After a few yards the lane forks and we go right passing a ruined cottage on the left and then take the left fork. Keeping on this tarmac drive we go through a spectacular avenue of cypress trees and out to a road where we turn left, noticing fine views on the left before the road becomes treelined. After about 100 yards at a point where the broken fence on the right ends and opposite a signposted stile on the left we turn right by a post and a large beech tree, then straight uphill through beech trees, where the path becomes more easily discernable. Eventually the path leads us out to a road and through posts where we turn left to the car park on our right.

(3)   If starting from Holmwood Station we walk back a short distance towards Dorking and at the last house on the left and at the 30 m.p.h. sign we turn left through a kissing gate along an enclosed path out to a lane where we turn left. After just over quarter of a mile at a fork we keep right going through a white gate and passing a pond down on the right, finally bearing right out to the road in which we turn right, soon passing the lodge of Kitlands on the left. Now continue at (2).

Refreshments: Available from the hut at the top of Leith Hill most weekends and fine days.

Headley Heath

Mickleham Downs, 5 miles

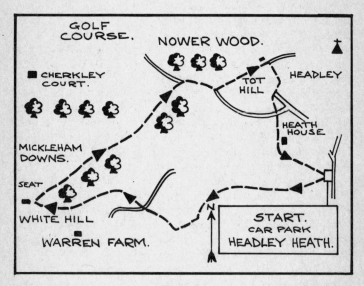

Walk 14

HERE are two walks from the car park on Headley Heath, the first walking over the Heath and Mickleham Downs, mostly on National Trust land, the other (Walk 15) in the opposite direction over farm fields, with optional visits to Headley and Walton churches and the village and pond at Walton. Both walks are pleasant, with bluebells in April and May and sweet chestnuts abounding in the autumn. Early in March in the woods near Headley Church, toothwort, a fairly uncommon parasite, can be seen growing round the roots of the hazel trees. The first walk is more spectacular, and is recommended for any time of the year.

The two walks form a figure of eight and the more energetic may wish to join the two together.

How to get there: By bus Nos 416 or 422 from Leatherhead Post Office, approximately an hourly service with no service on Sunday. By car on the B.2033.

At the mobile canteen by the car park we go forward across the heath with the road behind us, and cross an open space bearing slightly right, crossing a wide Horse Track and forward on a wide path, soon with a silver birch wood on the right and open heath on the left. We ignore all crossing tracks and on reaching a wide junction of 5 or 6 paths, continue in the same direction on a broad track with the woods on our right, soon coming to a small triangular open green space. We take the right fork, thus maintaining the same direction, on a grassy track ignoring all side turnings. This path becomes smaller as it goes downhill and bears left into trees. We then turn left with a wire fence on our right, noticing some splendid views of White Hill across the valley.

The path clings to a steeply sloping hillside following National Trust boundary posts on our right and then goes steeply down to the edge of the wood with a field on our right. Coming out of the woods into open heath we turn right into a main bridleway. In a very few yards, where we can see the end of the field through trees on our right, we turn sharply right into the trees and bear right up a steep path. At the top of the hill we turn right with the boundary wall of Wentworth Hall on our left. This path bears right and downhill eventually coming out to a road, Lodgebottom Road, with a cottage on the left.

Crossing the road to a footpath opposite we take the lower path at first parallel with the road. After about 300 yards at a junction of several paths and where our main path bears right, we keep straight ahead uphill under yew trees, ignoring the left fork with posts across. The woods here are a mixture of very fine beech trees and yews with an underplanting of box. After a further half a mile we emerge into open scrubland with a seat on the right and fine views of the north slopes of Boxhill. We turn right just before the seat, with a fence on our left. The path leaves the fence and turns right and we keep on this path for

53

perhaps 60 yards till on the left a path runs rather indistinctly between two beech trees, the right one of which leans heavily to the right. We take this path with open beech woods on the right and, at first, scrubby wood on the left. We bear slightly left with the path emerging on to the open space at the top of Mickleham Down. We turn right and continue for more than half a mile along this splendid grassy ride with lovely beech trees on the right.

At the end of the ride we enter the woods by a National Trust sign keeping along the fenced path with Surrey Naturalist Trust Nature Reserve on our right and later with open views of Headley Heath, eventually coming out through posts to a road. Here we turn right and at the end of the wood on our left take a bridleway on the left. Very soon we go over a stile on the right into a field with a wood on our left and bearing left round the edge of the wood. When the wood turns sharply left we keep straight on to a stile ahead, down a field with wire fencing on the left, over another stile, passing a house on the left, and over another stile in the left-hand corner into a lane, in which we turn right. The lane comes to a road and we again turn right passing a farm on the right. We keep straight on ignoring a left fork.

We are soon at a major road which we cross to the National Trust sign and take the left-hand one of two paths, going under a wooden bar and uphill. Soon the path forks and we go left continuing on through bracken until we have the thick holly hedge of Heath House on our left. As the hedge ends we cross a small tarmac drive and continue on a grassy path maintaining the same direction. Our path soon brings us out to a small open space with several paths turning off. We are now very close to the car park and if we maintain direction on any path we will soon be in sight of the car park and mobile canteen, but the easiest way is to take the second path on the right from this open space and then the first turning on the left and continue on the path through gorse and heather to the car park.

Refreshments available from the mobile canteen at Headley Heath car park.

Walton on the Hill

**Headley Heath and Walton on the Hill,
4 miles**

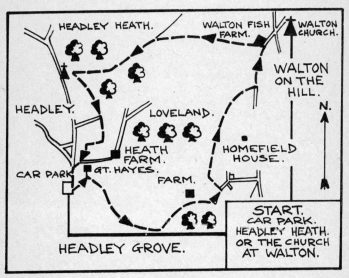

Walk 15

THE walk begins at Headley Heath car park but can be joined at Walton on a bus route. If starting the walk by bus we alight at the church and walk along the road following the bus route for a short distance turning right on the bridleway at the side of Walton Fish Farm.

We cross the road from the car park to the open space on the right of the cricket green, making for the rear of the cricket pavilion. This brings us out to a small tarmac road on which we turn right and after a few yards turn left up a drive leading to a house called Great Hayes. Just before the gate of Great Hayes we turn right on a path through the bracken, soon coming to a National Trust sign at a point where another path joins on the right. We maintain our direction on a path which is now bounded by trees on both sides. After a time this path becomes very muddy but there is a parallel path avoiding the mud at a slightly higher level on the right which will be helpful.

Eventually when the path forks, we take the left fork through open woods where deer have sometimes been seen. Later this path has open fields on the right and bears left to a tarmac crossing drive with farm buildings on the left. We turn left and in a few yards go through a kissing gate on the right at the beginning of an avenue of trees. The path is not visible on the ground but we cross the field diagonally right to a stile in a gap between trees. We cross the next field diagonally right towards trees which we leave on our left and continue in the same direction across the next field on a footpath clearly visible on the ground. This leads to a stile in a thick hedge and before us is a well kept sports field, adjacent to Howard Close and start of No. 80A bus route. We cross the sports field to a road in which we turn left into the outskirts of Walton. We go along the main road for a short distance and take a bridleway on the left by the side of Walton Fish Farm.

Walton church is a little further along the main road on the right. The churchyard has a yew tree 200 years old and though the church is not old it contains an 800-year-old lead font with worn figures in the Norman arches round it. The village street has many interesting antique shops and further down is the Withybed pond and several inns for refreshment.

We keep along this bridleway for just over half a mile, bearing left when another track feeds in from the right. Opposite a conifer plantation on the left we watch for a very distinct path on the right on which we bear uphill through woods to a fence and stile into a field. This field is often ploughed but we go straight across to Headley Church which can be seen ahead.

Again not an old church, the 14th century building was pulled down and some of the stones have been used to build a vault. The spire of Headley Church is a well-known landmark and can be seen for many miles around.

To continue the walk we do *not* go through the lych gate to the church but turn left. If the church is visited we then come back to this point.

We continue on this field path through gates and stiles for just under half a mile until the path turns sharply left and we can no longer go straight ahead. We then turn right over a stile, along the edge of a field, over another stile into a narrow footpath by the side of a house and then right to a road. Just before reaching the road, however, we turn left on to a small path in the trees running parallel with the road. At the private drive we turn right on to the main road, turning left for the car park.

Refreshments: Walton village and mobile canteen at Headley Heath car park.

Boxhill

(i) Boxhill, Duke's Plantation, Juniper Top 5½ miles
(ii) Boxhill, Brockham Railway Museum,
Betchworth Clump, The Whites 6½ miles

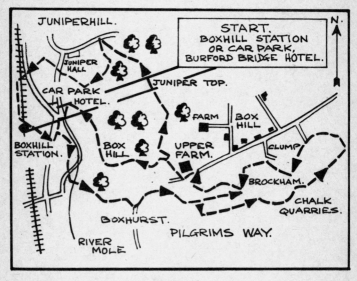

Walk 16

THE two different endings can be interchanged thus giving a short walk of 4¼ miles or a rather strenuous but rewarding walk of 7¾ miles.

These two walks will greatly increase our appreciation of the beauty of the Boxhill area. They are suitable for any time of the year but will give most pleasure in early summer when the chalk downland flowers and butterflies abound, or in the autumn when we can enjoy the changing colours of trees and shrubs. The longer walk takes us steeply uphill and downhill several times but it is an exciting walk and well worth the effort involved. It could be considered a good training course for anyone contemplating a walking holiday! It is not advisable to do it just after rain as the chalk slopes are slippery when wet.

How to get there: By No. 470 bus or Green Line Bus Nos. 712, 713 or 714 to Burford Bridge Hotel. By train to Boxhill Station. By car to the car park at Burford Bridge Hotel (one mile north of Dorking on the A.24).

For both walks
From the station. Leaving Boxhill Station we turn right down the road to the main road, crossing by the subway, turning left and immediately taking a small path on our right over a stile.

From the car park and Burford Bridge Hotel walk towards Dorking along the main road to the subway, just over the river bridge.

Once over the stile a grassy track takes us to the River Mole and we follow the riverside path with the steep wooded side of Boxhill towering above us. This is a beautiful stretch of the river, much frequented by fishermen of all ages. After some time our path bears right over a field and we cross the river by an iron bridge which was erected by The Ramblers Association in memory of their members who fell in the 1939-45 war. As an alternative we may go a little further along and cross by the stepping stones, but these are sometimes flooded.

Leaving the bridge we take the forward path away from the river and at a T junction in about 100 yards we turn left and uphill bearing right. As we mount upwards we can see splendid views on our right and it is useful to look out for blue waymarks on trees denoting the direction of our path. We keep upwards on the steep path, ignoring branching paths. At the top the path divides and we bear right, still following the blue waymarks. Our path is now somewhat enclosed in vegetation leading slightly uphill and finally out into the open.

We continue in the same direction on a small path around the contour of Boxhill with trees on our right and good views. In the summer this chalky downland area abounds in wild flowers and butterflies, particularly the beautiful chalkhill blue butterfly. Our path eventually turns slightly right, then forward and right again on a rough tree-lined track going downhill. This feeds into a road which we cross and turn left up a signposted footpath running parallel with the road.

For the shorter version

On this path we gain height and turn right on joining a flint bridleway which takes us round the side of the hill. After about a mile on this pleasant track we go round a sharp hairpin bend in an area known as Duke's Plantation and after rather less than half a mile, passing a red brick house on the left, we bear right out to the road. Here we turn left and are soon at Upper Farm Caravan site and swimming pool, with tea rooms on the left.

For the longer version

On this path we gain height and turn right on joining a flint bridleway which takes us round the side of the hill for half a mile. This track soon becomes open on our left and at the point where it becomes enclosed again in trees we immediately leave it and take a steep path by a wooden post downwards on our right under yew trees. At the bottom of the slope we turn left along a beautiful wide path with a yew wood sloping up on our left and a fringe of yews and open fields with a view of Brockham on our right.

Ignoring crossing tracks we continue in the same direction, past an old war time pill box on our right. This path leads us to a clearing used by the Brockham Museum Trust to house an interesting collection of ancient railway rolling stock. At weekends it is often possible to see enthusiastic volunteers engaged in clearance work, track laying and restoration work. The original narrow gauge track here was formerly used in connection with the old chalk quarries.

Our path continues on the other side of the railway clearing with disused lime kilns on our left and restored railway track on our right. We still keep at the base of the hill, on the lowest path just inside the edge of the wood, soon with open fields visible through the fringe of trees on our right. We continue for about half a mile, ignoring branching paths, and when our path is at a somewhat higher level and just before a large chimney of a disused lime quarry on on our right, our path takes a sudden left turn to a higher level. In a few yards at a crossing track we turn right noticing that the disused chimney stack which we pass on our right actually has bushes and a small tree growing out of the top. We go over a bridge and our path soon crosses a rough chalk track and continues slightly downwards and across a wide chalk road leading to quarry workings on our left. We continue, passing a row of cottages on the left, and at a junction turn left into a lane which soon turns sharply right, while we go through posts on our left into an uphill footpath. This is a steep climb up-hill around the Betchworth Clump but taken slowly it gives splendid views when stopping for breath. The path bears left and still uphill through trees but eventually flattens out, coming to a signpost.

We keep forward with a reservoir building on our right, and come out into a small open space which is a good picnic spot with spectacular views overlooking the quarry. On the other side of the clearing, we take a small path with the hill sloping down on our left, go through some open beeches and just past a Surrey County Council notice, *Betchworth Clump* we take the left fork, going slightly downhill on a path through trees, cling-ing to the hillside. Eventually we come out into the open and go downhill much more steeply between young yew trees, to a well defined chalky crossing track. Here we turn right and proceed gently uphill. Walking at the top of the left-hand bank gives the best views. Among the trees on our left below the hill, a small lake formed from a disused quarry, can be seen.

We keep to the main path and at the top where the bank is supported by corrugated fencing we turn left uphill to visit a grave stone on our right inscribed ' "Quick". 26.9.36 to 22.10.44. An English thoroughbred'.

We continue past the grave on our right on a small footpath with a caravan site on our right and after a while our path joins a wide bridleway in which we turn left.

This track soon goes steeply downhill giving some fine views on our left through the trees. There are some wooden steps across the path from time to time and at the eleventh step we turn sharply right and steeply uphill into trees. This path soon comes out to the wide flint bridleway through Duke's Plantation at the hairpin bend. We take the right and slightly uphill arm and continue along it, finally passing a red brick house on the left and bearing right to the road in which we turn left to Upper Farm Caravan Site.

For both walks we have a choice of two ways back to Burford Bridge Hotel

(a)   *Over "The Whites" 1½ miles*

At Upper Farm Caravan site we turn right and walk in the woods with the caravan park on our right. It is necessary to keep our wits about us owing to the large number of paths. At the end of the fence and caravan park we go straight ahead on a wide path, ignoring a similar track on the right which bears right. After 50 yards we take a left fork and keep on this main track. Shortly after the point where other paths join it and this main track bears left, we turn sharp left on a well defined path. At the fork in about 50 yards we keep right and go through a clearing with a wooden hut on the left, bearing right at the end of the clearing and shortly, at a crossing track, again turn right. In approximately 150-200 yards, at a faint crossing track, our track forks and we go left between beech trees. After a few yards our track bears left, still through beech trees, and after 50 yards or so, at a wide crossing track, we turn left then straight ahead to an open green space at the top of Boxhill, without crossing the road. We cross the open space, bearing right to the Fort Tea Rooms where we cross the road. We leave the Tea Rooms and a telephone kiosk on our left and when this path forks it does not matter which fork we take, one goes past old fortifications and they both come out to the well-known white chalk track over the top of Boxhill. Noticing the views of Ranmore Common and Ranmore church spire ahead, we go downhill on the ridge towards a red tiled house, and nearing the foot of the hill we bear left to the car park and Burford Bridge Hotel.

(b)   *Over Juniper Top, Fredley and Boxhill Station 2¾ miles*

We leave the road by taking a path at the side of the caravan site and at the end of the boundary fence we maintain direction, past a beech tree, going left at a fork, continuing on and ignoring branching paths. We come to a large round bushy yew tree on our right at a crossing track and a red waymark on a tree on the left and ignore one more crossing track, continuing downhill for about 150 yards when we take a small path on our right going slightly uphill. This path through box, yew and beech is especially beautiful when it comes out into the open, giving views across the valley of Juniper Bottom. When our path re-enters a wooded area we can still catch glimpses of views but later we are in a more enclosed yew wood, eventually emerging into the open on Juniper Top, with fine views of Mickleham Downs straight ahead and Ranmore Common in the distance. We keep to the open space in the centre of this shoulder of hill and continue downhill on a gradual slope, with thick trees, mostly yews, on our left, and later birch trees. Continuing down the shoulder of the hill at the bottom the path enters a wooded area and we come out under a wooden bar into Juniper Bottom, where we turn left, doubling back along the valley. On our right we have a field behind trees, and then a small wooded area. Just before an open slope we take a narrow path into woods. This is *not* the path outside the wood with the open space on the left.

Alternatively from Juniper Top it is possible to take a short cut down to Juniper Bottom and save about a quarter of a mile. Soon after yew trees on the left give way to silver birches, we leave the broad green centre track and go along a smaller path with the birches immediately on our left. At a point where there is a single birch tree on our right there is a narrow path on the left which winds down to Juniper Bottom by the wood and open space.

The path in the woods soon goes steeply uphill and comes to the boundary fence of National Trust property which we keep on our right, noticing Juniper Hall, also on our right, at the bottom of the sloping meadow.

Our track goes downhill past a house, Pinehurst, on our left, through the trees, and finally winds down to a road which we cross, taking a side road opposite and bearing right. On this pleasant private road we soon pass Fredley Barn on our right and we take a small fenced path on the left at the side of a bungalow leading down to the main A.24 road, which we cross with care, taking a path immediately ahead.

This leads us under a railway bridge, where we bear left and go over a bridge crossing the River Mole, continuing on a grassy path with the railway embankment on our left. A stile takes us to an enclosed path leading to the road where we turn left to Boxhill Station a few yards away, or continue down the road to the main road and Burford Bridge Hotel.

Refreshments: The tea rooms at Upper Farm or Fort Tea Rooms at the top of Boxhill.

Reigate Hill

**Reigate Hill, Colley Hill
4½ or 6¾ miles**

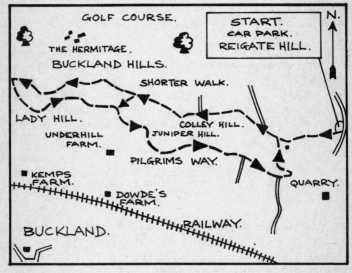

Walk 17

IN THIS walk we explore the breezy open slopes of Reigate and Colley Hill with wide panoramic views, continuing along Juniper Hill, Buckland Hills and Lady Hill and returning along the ancient trackway at the foot of the range of hills. While being enjoyable at any season, this walk is particularly beautiful in autumn when the beeches at the foot of Colley Hill are changing colour. After winter rains, the lower paths become rather muddy in places and the steep path down through the Buckland Hills, for the shorter walk, should be avoided in rainy conditions.

How to get there: By Green Line bus No. 711 or Green No. 406 bus to the top of Reigate Hill. By car to car park at the top of Reigate Hill on A.217.

From the car park we make for the footbridge over the main road, passing the refreshment hut and toilets on our right. We follow this tree lined track for about three quarters of a mile, passing a water tower on our right, and coming out at the open top and memorial fountain of Colley Hill.

Noticing the slopes of Leith Hill in the distance we continue along this grassy hill top through sundry clumps of hawthorn and yew and eventually come to a National Trust sign, *Colley Hill.* Keeping in the same direction along the hill top path, between a wire fence on our left and shrubs on the right, we pass through three sets of posts, keeping left and ignoring branching paths. We soon come out on to a small tarmac road where we turn left and right again almost at once on a path next to an iron gate marked with the names of two houses and a sign saying *Strictly Private.* We are now walking along the top of Juniper Hill on a rather enclosed path but in winter and spring giving good views on the left from time to time. Emerging at a house named Conybury Heights, we have the choice of either a short or long walk.

For the short walk

By Conybury Heights is a "squeeze" leading into a narrow footpath with a holly hedge on the right and wire fence on the left, taking us down through the Buckland Hills. At the end of the fence we go through yews and soon very steeply downhill, coming suddenly out into the open with wonderful views. We continue downhill towards a clump of trees and just before the bottom turn left on a crossing track which is part of the ancient trackway running along the foot of this range of hills.

For the long walk

At Conybury Heights we continue forward in the same direction and are soon walking on the top of the Buckland Hills, still on an enclosed path, with the back of an occasional house on the left and open fields visible through the fringe of trees on our right. The path enters a wooded area which is undoubtedly muddy in winter or wet weather, but there are occasional paths avoiding the mud on either side of the main track, which soon bears left and emerges into the open, giving fine views of the Betchworth Clump, with the Redlands heights and the side slopes of Leith Hill in the distance. On a clear day the South Downs are visible on the horizon.

Continuing with a fenced wood on our right, the path soon turns left for a short way downhill and then right again, thus skirting a rectangular field by turning right up the third side of the field. We are now on Lady Hill. Our path leaves the rectangular field at a signpost and bears left into woods, turning uphill and out to a wide bridleway along the highest part of the hill, where we turn left, with the woods on our left.

Soon our wide track turns sharply right and we take a downward path on our left. Almost at once there are left and right forks leading off but we ignore these and continue downwards with steep banks on either side. Our path, bordered by ancient yews, bears left, giving good views on our right and sometimes glimpses of a white chalk cliff on our left.

At the point where a line of pylons in the open field on our right is very close to our path, we take a small track leading upwards on our left. This path leads round the base of the hills over which we have walked and gives good views. Soon we are walking on an open path through an area noted in summer for its variety of wild flowers and butterflies.

We continue forward at the foot of the hills, sometimes in the open and sometimes under trees and on the left a small path comes down from the Buckland Hills to join our path, while a right fork leads to Underhill Farm.

Both walks now follow the same route:
We eventually come out under a wooden bar and National Trust sign indicating we have just walked round the foot of Juniper Hill. We continue past another National Trust sign, *Colley Hill,* going under a bar into an avenue of yew trees and following the path which twists and turns around the base of the hill.

At Colley Pits we ignore a fork on our left and go down some steps, still keeping along the foot of the hill ignoring all turnings off to the right. We finally come out into a tarmac road and go under a wooden barrier still maintaining our direction. In about 100 yards as the road turns right we fork left to a house, "Underbeeches", and turn sharply left again with a beech hedge on the left and wall on the right. This path soon becomes rutted and chalky, giving views on the left. We continue uphill to a granite memorial obelisk and when the track levels out we turn right up some steps which bring us back to the memorial fountain on Colley Hill which we passed earlier. Turning right we retrace our steps along the bridleway back to the car park.

Refreshments: The hut in the car park at the top of Reigate Hill.

Chipstead Valley

Chipstead Valley and Long Plantation
4½ miles

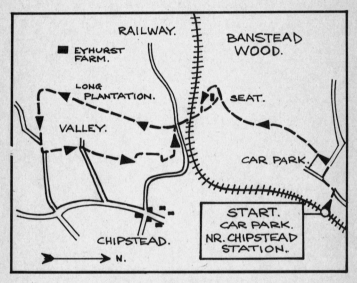

Walk 18

THIS walk is in a delightful area very close to London with wild flowers on the hillside and good views across the valley.

How to get there: By train to Chipstead station, going down Station Approach, and turning left in main road to the car park. By bus Nos. 166 or 166A to Chipstead Valley, alighting at *The Midday Sun,* walking along Outwood Lane to Holly Lane. By car to the Banstead Woods car park at the end of Holly Lane, B.2219.

Starting from the car park with our backs to Holly Lane we go through a kissing gate on the extreme left and uphill to a path on the *outside* of Banstead Woods. This path is uphill at first, giving fine views on the left, and we remain on it for about a mile, without entering the woods on the right.

When our path forks we go left and are soon out on the open hillside with an open field on our right and fringe of trees and downward slope on our left. When the railway viaduct is in sight on our left we watch out for a large beech tree on our right and go forward a few yards to a seat and a junction of three paths. We take the path on the extreme right with open woods on the right and a valley with fine views on our left. Soon our path enters an open beech wood by a seat and after 20 yards we take a small path on the left which doubles back at a lower level. This is a small deviation to enjoy really fine views and we have soon joined the path which was on the extreme left at the recent junction of three paths. We continue downhill across the railway and are soon out to the road which we cross bearing slightly left to a stile with a footpath sign.

We go forward with a garden fence on our right but as the fence turns a corner we maintain direction and bear right up a slope to a stile which takes us through a narrow strip of woods and out to a field. We bear right uphill round the edge of this field to a stile with a Surrey County Council notice indicating that we are entering an area known as Long Plantation. Crossing the stile we turn left on a path through this beautiful open wood which consists mainly of yew and beech trees, with good views across the valley on the left. When the path forks, either fork may be used as the left fork soon rejoins the main path. After about three quarters of a mile on the path in Long Plantation we come to a T junction where we turn left, crossing the valley on a wide track and up to a stile and a road where we turn left uphill for about 50 yards to another footpath on the left which leads us back along the other side of the valley.

When our path is joined by a track coming in on the right we continue in a forward direction with woods on our right and open valley on our left. When we have practically completed our return on the other side of the valley we take a stile at the side of a gate, maintain direction across an open field and then bear left downhill on a footpath which leads us back to the stile and road which we crossed earlier.

We now retrace our steps, crossing the railway and continuing straight up our uphill path, ignoring a path on the left, to the seat at the top where we turn right and return along the path outside Banstead Woods to the car park.

Refreshments and toilet facilities available at the car park.

Coulsdon

Coulsdon, Happy Valley and Chaldon
5 miles (or alternatively 3¼ miles from the Welcome Tea Rooms)

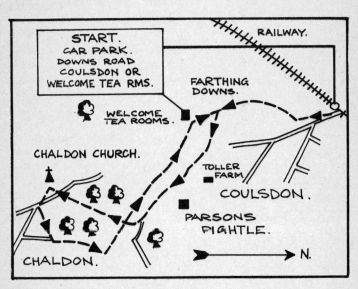

Walk 19

THIS is a lovely area very close to London where wild flowers abound and through careful clearing many rarer plants are beginning to appear on the chalky slopes in the valley. The woods are a beautiful sight in May with bluebells, red campion and white stitchwort.

How to get there: By bus Nos. 190 or 59 to Downs Road, Coulsdon, via any bus which goes along Marlpit Lane. Cars may be parked at the beginning of Downs Road, or alternatively at the top of the downs by the Welcome Tea Rooms.

There are many tracks going south over Farthing Downs and a small tarmac road for cars. For the best views and to avoid the sight of cars we keep to the side slopes well over to the right where the Downs Road houses are partly screened by a fringe of yew trees. At the end of Downs Road we turn left up a grassy track which leads uphill to the highest part of Farthing Downs where there are two trees, a signpost and a seat. Here we turn right along a well kept wide grassy track on the top of the Downs. We ignore two crossing tracks and soon the area known as Happy Valley can be seen ahead on the left. We are well within sight of the Welcome Tea Rooms when our grassy track ends and we turn left through wooden posts and down the shoulder of the Downs on a bridleway which bears right into a wooded area. As the bridleway bears left and downhill we maintain our direction by going under a wooden bar and proceeding on a narrow path which takes us downhill through a small wood and out into the open.

We are now at the bottom of the valley and we continue forward along the valley bottom with woods on our right and upward slopes with some trees on the left. As a wide track leads uphill on the left we continue forward keeping along the bottom of the valley. We pass a second track going uphill on the left and in about half a mile we come to a hedge which spans the valley.

Here we turn right uphill, over a stile, through a strip of woodland and over an open field on a well defined track bearing slightly left. When this wide track crosses a second field the spire of Chaldon church comes into sight directly ahead. When our track reaches the other side of the field it bears away to the left but we bear slightly uphill to a footpath signpost and out on to the road where we turn left and right almost at once on a small approach road leading to St. Peter and St. Paul's Church, Chaldon.

This ancient church, which dates back to 1100, contains many treasures, such as a tomb 600 years old, and a tablet inscribed in 1562, but chief among these is the unique and remarkable mural painted in 1170 but only discovered in 1870 under a preserving coat of whitewash.

Leaving the church by the other approach road on the right we go down to the road which we cross to a signposted footpath on a grassy track with open fields on the left and backs of houses on the right. Soon we have a wood on our left but we remain on the outside of the wood until we reach a crossing lane where we turn left with the wood still on our left and houses and gardens on the right. At the last house the lane becomes a footpath and enters the wood sloping slightly downhill for about quarter of a mile until the valley becomes visible on our left.

Here we leave our track which continues downhill while we go under a wooden bar turning left along the open hillside with woods on our left. We are soon back at the hedge which spans the valley and we pass through a gap keeping up on the hillside with woods on our left and the valley bottom on our right. Our path takes us through a small wooded strip and out into the open again and we maintain direction. We re-enter the woods and our wide track soon leads us out to the Welcome Tea Rooms and toilets on our left. After refreshment we retrace our steps along Farthing Downs back to the car park and bus stop at Downs Road.

Refreshments: Welcome Tea Rooms at the top of Farthing Downs.

Chelsham

**Chelsham, Woldingham and back
6¾ miles**

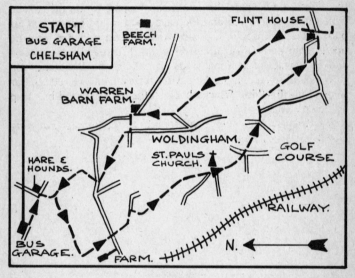

Walk 20

THIS is a pleasant summer walk with plenty of chalkland flowers and butterflies on the downs and the field footpaths. Some mud will be encountered in places more especially in the wetter months.

How to get there: By bus to Chelsham bus garage, Green bus No. 483 or Green Line bus No. 706. There is ample car parking space nearby.

We leave Chelsham bus garage and turn right along High

Lane just past *The Hare and Hounds,* shortly turning right along Plantation Lane continuing on the main track straight ahead with the valley down on the left. After just over half a mile we take the first stile on the left near a farm down in the valley and go straight across the field to another stile at the end of a straggly line of pine trees. Keeping straight ahead we make for another stile to the right of more trees ahead. Crossing the road to a stile opposite we go straight up the hill to a stile under trees, through a strip of wood and out to a small residential road. Here we turn left and as the road turns left we go straight ahead on a footpath between beech and privet hedges, crossing another small road, continuing forward, then down a stepped path to a crossing track. We turn left along here and for about half a mile we enjoy a well made path with occasional seats, woods on our left and a valley on our right with good views. The last part of the path is fenced and eventually comes out to a wider lane where we turn left to St. Paul's church, Woldingham.

Built in 1933, this church is well worth a visit. The bluish agates set in the inscription above the altar were a gift from Hyderabad, and the stained glass windows above the altar depict the sea in various moods. The roof timbers of Columbian pine support concealed lighting and the windows are surrounded with dressed flints.

Leaving the church on our left we continue along the road to Woldingham Green and turn left down Upper Court Road. Just past a house called Sylvan Mount we turn left down a steep path, passing a house on the right at the bottom of the dip. We cross the crossing track and go up Southview Road and just past a house turn slightly left to a signposted footpath.

We follow this path for about half a mile, at first along the edge of trees and finally uphill with trees eventually on our left, and over stiles out to a road. We cross over and turn left to admire the view over Oxted from the old road, following it to a road junction where we take the road signposted Oxted and Limpsfield. We continue on this road for a short distance then take a footpath on the left downhill to the top of the downs for views and a rest.

Retracing our steps back to the road we turn right and back to the cross roads and cross over to Flint House Lane, the bridleway to Warlingham, passing Flint House on the left. We continue straight ahead along this bridleway for a good mile. The last half mile of the path has woods on our right and is often rather muddy, but we eventually emerge at the top of a wide sloping field and go downhill on a clear path and out to the road.

Here we turn right passing some elegant houses and opposite Warren Barn Farm we turn left along Upland Road. At the T junction we turn right along a pleasant residential road out to Slines Oak Road. Here we turn left and almost immediately right along High Lane which takes us uphill and finally back to a green space opposite the bus garage.

Refreshments: Confectionery and ice cream at Woldingham village and Chelsham